YOUR KNOWLEDGE HAS VALUE

- We will publish your bachelor's and master's thesis, essays and papers

- Your own eBook and book - sold worldwide in all relevant shops

- Earn money with each sale

Upload your text at www.GRIN.com
and publish for free

Bibliographic information published by the German National Library:

The German National Library lists this publication in the National Bibliography; detailed bibliographic data are available on the Internet at http://dnb.dnb.de .

This book is copyright material and must not be copied, reproduced, transferred, distributed, leased, licensed or publicly performed or used in any way except as specifically permitted in writing by the publishers, as allowed under the terms and conditions under which it was purchased or as strictly permitted by applicable copyright law. Any unauthorized distribution or use of this text may be a direct infringement of the author s and publisher s rights and those responsible may be liable in law accordingly.

Imprint:

Copyright © 2014 GRIN Verlag
Print and binding: Books on Demand GmbH, Norderstedt Germany
ISBN: 9783668653245

This book at GRIN:

https://www.grin.com/document/414625

Moges Endalamaw Yigermal

The Determinants of Academic Performance of Under Graduate Students

Case of Arba Minch University Chamo Campus

GRIN Verlag

GRIN - Your knowledge has value

Since its foundation in 1998, GRIN has specialized in publishing academic texts by students, college teachers and other academics as e-book and printed book. The website www.grin.com is an ideal platform for presenting term papers, final papers, scientific essays, dissertations and specialist books.

Visit us on the internet:

http://www.grin.com/

http://www.facebook.com/grincom

http://www.twitter.com/grin_com

Advances in Sciences and Humanities
2017; 3(4): 35-42
http://www.sciencepublishinggroup.com/j/ash
doi: 10.11648/j.ash.20170304.12

The Determinants of Academic Performance of Under Graduate Students: In the Case of Arba Minch University Chamo Campus

Moges Endalamaw Yigermal

College of Business and Economics, Arba Minch University, Arba Minch, Ethiopia

Email address:
Mogeshabesha@gmail.com, gebre09meskel@gmail.com

To cite this article:
Moges Endalamaw Yigermal. The Determinants of Academic Performance of Under Graduate Students: In the Case of Arba Minch University Chamo Campus. *Advances in Sciences and Humanities.* Vol. 3, No. 4, 2017, pp. 35-42. doi: 10.11648/j.ash.20170304.12

Received: March 30, 2017; **Accepted:** April 25, 2017; **Published:** August 30, 2017

Abstract: The main objective of the paper is to investigate the determinant factors affecting the academic performance of regular undergraduate students of Arba Minch university (AMU) chamo campus students. To meet the objective, the Pearson product moment correlation statistical tool and econometrics data analysis (OLS regression) method were used with the aim of establishing the relationship between factors related to student's background and family background on academic performance of regular undergraduate students at Arba Minch university chamo campus students. The findings proved the existence of significant relationship between gender difference, university entrance exam, studying hours and academic performance (CGPA). The findings also revealed that there was a significant relationship between students former academic back ground, studying hours, and student's behavior on taking of alcoholic drug and chat on academic performance of students. On the basis of the findings, the researcher recommended that emphasis should be taken to improve the academic performance of female students, working at the ground with high school students earlier before they joined in to university and Providing Psychotherapy and supporting alcoholic drug and khat taker students to end the use such drug and Khat will bring more fruit to improve students' academic performance.

Keywords: Academic Performance, Determinant, OLS Regression

1. Introduction

1.1. Back Ground of the Study

Beyond any doubt education plays a pivotal role in the development and progress of a country. In a developing country education gains even more importance.

The issue of poor academic performance of students in developing countries has been much concern at all. In developing countries the problem of poor academic performance leads to the widely acclaimed fallen standard of education. Government investment on higher education and its output in terms of student's achievement good performance of students has been observed to be unequal with government expenditure. Most of the developing countries are improving their system in an effort to increase their tertiary student's enrollment ratio [1].

Ethiopia possesses a 1700 year tradition of elite education linked to the Orthodox Church. But secular higher educations were initiated in the year 1950 with the founding of university college of Addis Ababa [2]. Now a time the Ethiopian government has long recognized to the realization of higher education as a necessity and fundamental human development of the country and also the number of both governmental and nongovernmental higher institutions increased enough as compared with previous situations. In the year 2005 E. C. (2012/13) the total undergraduate enrolment (government and non-government; regular, evening, summer and distance programs) is 553,848 of which 166, 141 are females which accounts for 30% of the total enrolment. In addition, 474,198 (85.6%) of the total undergraduate enrolment is in government institutions. undergraduate enrolment is highest in regular programs and lowest in distance programs. The distance program is the only program in which the non-government undergraduate enrolment is higher than the government enrolment. The regular program accounts for 57.4% of total undergraduate enrolment.

Ethiopian undergraduate student's enrollment trend in regular program shows an increasing trend over time. For instance in the year 2001/2008/09 the total number of students in rolled in regular undergraduate level was counted as 157424, of the total students enrolled as an undergraduate female students account 28.95% while the remaining 71.1% were male students. And also in the year 2004/2011/2012 the number of regular students enrolled as regular undergraduate program increased by 92805 or to 250229 [3].

As far as Arba Minch University is concerned in the year 2001/2007/08 the number of undergraduate students enrolled in regular program was 10766, of the total number of students enrolled as undergraduate female students account 33.6% and the remaining 66% covered by male students. The enrollment statistics of the year 2004/2011/12 student's enrollment number increased by 17.9% or to 13111. And also in the year 2005 E. C. (2012/13) the total undergraduate student's enrolment is increased to 14,438 Which 11,063 are males and 3,375 are female. So the trend indicates that enrollment of undergraduate student's increases time to time [3].

1.2. Statement of the Problem

Students' academic gain and learning performance is affected by numerous factors including gender, teaching faculty, students previous education background, students behavior of taking drug including chat, families social, educational and economic status and soon. In Ethiopia there is a quite public investment in the school system more over the increase in the number of students in higher education is a national goal that have been pursued by education policy. For instance Public spending on education, which during the 1980s remained under 10% of total spending, had increased to 23.6% of total expenditure by 2008/09. This constitutes 5.5% of gross domestic product (GDP), one of the highest rates on the continent [4].

However in spite of all the excessive government investment, failure to achieve a good performance is a major problem that affects all level of education. At university level failure to achieve a good performance affects many undergraduate students. This problem is a major concern for those involved in higher education [4].

The number of students in Arba Minch University enrolled as undergraduate regular program increase time to time. For instance in the year 2001/2001/07 number of undergraduate enrolled as regular undergraduate was 1,0766 and after three years number of students enrolled as regular under graduate program increased to 1,3111. Despite the increasing trend of the enrollment of students, the number of students graduating there by completing the required training tends to increase less proportionally to the enrollment trend and many students fail to achieve good performance and withdrawal from campus or commit readmission.

Since Poor performance of students at university level is a major issue it needs much concern. More of the previous studies focus on primary education level but the problem is not addressed well at university level and much previous research's conducted abroad. And also in Arba Minch University there is no well-organized study conducted on this problem. So this study primarily designed to fill this gap and conducted to examine factors affecting student's academic performance at undergraduate level and also try to give insight about the effect of those factors on academic achievement of students or students CGPA.

1.3. Objective and Scope of the Study

The scope of the study is bounded on the determining factors affect the academic performance of undergraduate students in Arba Minch university Chamo campus in 2014. Specifically the paper try's to address the following objectives:-

(1) To examine differences in academic performance of students across gender.
(2) To examine the effect of student's former academic performance background on academic achievement at university level.
(3) To explore the effect of family education and income back ground on students' academic performance /GPA.
(4) To assess the effect of students behavior in taking of alcohol and chat and sexual partnership status on their academic performance.

1.4. Working Hypothesis

The researcher hypothesis important variables as:
(1) Students former school back ground performance positively affects CGPA at university level
(2) students behavior on taking alcoholic drug and chat negatively affects students' academic performance
(3) family education and income background positively affects students' performance

2. Literature Review

This section presents both theoretical and empirical literature reviews of related studies.

2.1. Theoretical Literature Review

Undergraduate programs are offered for three, four or more years after completing secondary education. Completion of this program is certified by awarding a bachelor's degree. Undergraduate graduates are those who completed their study at the higher education institutions, and were awarded a bachelor's or first degree.

Higher education and economic development in sub-Saharan Africa.

Education is widely accepted as a leading instrument for promoting economic growth. For Africa, where growth is essential if the continent is to climb out of poverty, education is particularly important. Higher education is a determinant as well as a result of income, and can produce public and private benefits.4 Higher education may create greater tax revenue, increase savings and investment, and lead to a more entrepreneurial and civic society. It can also improve a nation's health, contribute to reduced population growth, and improve technology, and strengthen governance.

Higher education and economic development in Ethiopia

Ethiopia is currently engaged in highly ambitious effort to re-align its higher education system in more direct support of its national strategy for economic growth and poverty reduction. Its achievement over the past five years has been impressive, and an aggressive expansion policy designed to raise the countries insignificant tertiary enrollment ratio to more respectable levels.

Poverty alleviation in Ethiopia requires sustained economic growth, good governance and political stability in order to be effective. Growth drives from skilled human resource and national productivity increases leading to greater country competitiveness in regional as well as global economy. Productivity gains are generated by national innovation system in which tertiary education institutions play fundamental role. This institution determines levels of capability with in the country's pool of higher level of managerial, scientific and technological experts. The effectiveness with which global knowledge is accessed and applied in the solution of local development problems and the standard of quality with in lower level of education. The quality of secondary school teachers has a direct relation of the quality of training they receive in universities. Therefore if poverty is to be reduced Ethiopia's tertiary institutions will have to improve their performance and expand their service delivery. Specifically they must operate more effectively under service resource constraints and orient themselves to demands of the knowledge economy and to the growing emphasis on national capacity building. Higher education development combined with strategic development of the economy and labor force. It can contribute to job creation and productivity there by expands resource and opportunities for the poor people [5].

Government investment on education in Ethiopia

Total education spending, public and private, as share of GDP, is relatively high in Ethiopia, given its level of per-capita income and public spending accounts for over 90% of the total. However, the composition of public education spending is relatively top heavy, with higher education absorbing 40% of the total during 2005-08 which share is estimated to have risen above 50% during 2008-10 [4].

Worldwide Trend of school drop out

Drop out is a serious existing problem; it describes an excused absence from lessons. The problem cannot be related upon and reviewed by restricted perspective focusing only on school and lessons. Drop out also defined as breaking off from schooling for the rest of the term without a final certification, death and changing school excluded. Drop out also can be expressed as people who fail outside the usual parameters given by society.

Official data gathered by UNESCO proves that from a selection of sub-Saharan countries with a higher drop out and repetition rate are Chad, Mozambique Mauritian, and Benin shows a higher dropout rate in both sex than Ethiopia.

Higher education's students drop out in the world considered as those how had left higher education program and withdraw during their higher education study. Drop out / attrition/ can be measured by dismissed or academic failure and withdraw. Drop out is a worldwide problem, but the magnitude or the trend varies between developing and developed countries. A report developed by UNISCO on 88 developing countries shows those 30% students dropout from higher education registered in developing countries. And the national dropout rate in higher education for developing countries accounts on average 12% annually.

2.2. Empirics

This section presents determinants of academic performance of college students explained by previous researchers.

The study of [6] found that high school grade point average is consistently the best predictor of college grade of students. And also the same study held by Anderson, Benjamin and fuss (1994) carried out a study on the determinants of success in university and found out that students performed better in high school also performs better in college and the researcher suggested that high school grades were predictors of academic performance at college without doubt.

A study by [8] on the influence of social and economic disadvantage in the academic performance of school students in Australia found that families where parents are advantaged socially, economically and educationally foster a higher a higher level of achievement in their children. They also found that parents provide higher level of psychological support for their children through environments that encourage the development of skill necessary for success at school. And they pointed out that low social economic status of families negatively affect academic achievement of children's because of low socio economic status prevents access to vital resources and creates additional stress at home.

Research by [6] on determinant of academic performance shows significant relationship between former school back ground and academic performance of undergraduate students. The regression result of the study shows that significant relationship between former school background and academic performance of undergraduate students. The Pearson product moment correlation coefficient index (r) a significant correlation or p-value prevails 0.000 which is less than alpha (0.01) hence this indicates that there is a significant relationship between former school background of students and academic performance at undergraduate level.

A study conducted by [9] using primary research and analyzing data for secondary and tertiary level institutions asserted that male students generally under achievement than female students. He further explains that

Research conducted in Zimbabwe analysis that variables

such as gender, age, environment and access to internet explained or determine the academic performance of undergraduate students. Based on to the results obtained from this study gender gaps in favor of male student's better performance than females students in academic achievement.

A study conducted by [9] indicates that the significant relationship between priori educational success of students and their academic performance at undergraduate level and also the analysis proofs the direct relationship between parent's socio economic background and impacts of friend on academic achievement.

A research carried out a study by [10] on determinates of student performance at university reflections from the Caribbean analyze their study on 900 samples students and the econometric result shows that gender gap in favor of male students is only related with university entrance exam scores. But in undergraduate level female students score high grade or perform better than males. The researcher pointed out the reason that female students perform or score low grade in entrance exam result and they joined in less competitive departments and this situations makes female students perform better or score high CGPA in undergraduate level than male students.

A study carried out by [12] on the determinant of academic performance hec- lausane graduates using tobit model and he analysis econometrically the relationship between different variables related with personal and family backgrounds and average mark of students and he conclude that socio economic background of family and good personal background of students contribute to better academic achievement.

A study by [11] on determinants of academic performance of students uses multi-logit method of analysis on money and banking courses and with a sample of 97 students. The regression result indicates that college entrance exam and student's attendance determines academic performance. A student who attends attentively in class performs better in academic achievement.

A study conducted by [5] on undergraduate students of economics in Osun state indicates that family structure have great influence on academic performance of undergraduate students. According to this study family income and educational levels of parents as well as entrance exam of students determine student's achievement in education. Students from illiterate parents perform less than students from literate. This infers socio economic background of parents is an impetus to academic growth and performance of students.

An article conducted by [17] on The Determinants of Student Attrition at College of Business and Economics, Mekelle University: Econometric Investigation indicates that student's gender, national entrance examination overall results and mother education level significantly correlate with student performance. Female students found to perform lower than male students. Student's national entrance examination overall result is positively correlated with the student performance which is in line with our expectation. Those Students who do not drink alcohol found to have better academic performance than otherwise. Student's mother educational background significantly affects student CGPA, i.e. the higher the level of mother education in years the better the student to perform keeping other things the same. For Public and Development Management students we found student's gender, age and financial constraint to negatively affect academic performance. We also found that national entrance examination overall results and Mathematics result significantly affect student performance. Study hours per day and father education also positively affect student academic performance.

A research carried out by [13] on factors affecting female students academic achievement at Bahir Dar university. They take a sample of 600 students on second year and above undergraduate female students and the result that they obtained shows that academic achievement of female students affected by students personal related factors such as less ability to competent, tension, failing in love easily, being addicted to drinking, smoking, disco houses etc. university related factors such as, influence of male students, lack of proper guidance, lack of proper reading place where students use freely, influence from male teachers and youth from surrounding environment.

3. Research Methodology

3.1. Model Specification

While specifying the model, the researcher takes in to consideration important variables indicated by other researchers in determining students' academic performance. Moreover, the present study includes additional variables that are not indicated by previous scholars such as; the effect of sexual partnership and studying hours of students on their academic achievement.

Accordingly, the linear model can be written as:-

$$CGPA = B0 + B1AGE + B2GEN + B3AP + B4FPEM + B5ME + B6FE + B7PI + B8BTAC + B9SEX + B10 + HS + Ui \quad (1)$$

Where,

$B1 > 0, B2 > 0, B3 > 0, B4 > 0, B5 > 0, B6 > 0, B7 > 0, B8 < 0, B9 < 0, B10 > 0$

3.2. Variable Descriptions

Table 1. List of variables Used in the model.

List of variables	Description	Notation
Age	age of the respondent	Age
Gender	Sex of the respondent	GEN
Admission point in to the university	University result of the respondent	AP
Former proficiency of English and mathematics courses	Students entrance exam English and mathematics courses results	FPEM
Mother's Education	Education level of female guardian /mothers of respondent	ME
Fathers education	Education level of male guardian /fathers of respondent	FE
Parental Income	Parental income of respondent	PI
Behaviour of taking alcoholic drug and chat	Behaviour of students in taking of alcoholic drug and chat of respondent	BTAC
Sexual partnership	Sexual partnership of the respondent	SEX
Studying hours	Studying hours of the respondent	HS
Residual	unexplained part of the model	U

3.2.1. Data and Sampling Design

The study uses both primary and secondary source of data. Primary data has been collected from the selected sample students from each academic department trough questionnaire and structured interview. Secondary data or List of the selected samples from each department has been acquired from Chamo campus registrar office or departmental office.

Because of the heterogeneity nature of the population included in the study the representative sample students selected from each department through stratified sampling techniques. The study assumes each department as strata and sample have been selected from each stratum. Among 1309 total number of second year and above undergraduate students the representative samples are 100. And the representative sample is selected from each department or strata.

3.2.2. Method of Data Analysis

To meet the objective, Econometrics method of data analysis has been used to explain the inferential relationship between academic performance of student's /CGPA/ and determinant factors of academic performance. Ordinary least square (OLS) has been used to determine the value of parameters and estimating of the model.

4. Result and Discussion

Table 2. Respondent's academic performance by their cumulative grade point average (CGPA).

Students performance	(LP) CGPA<2.49	(HP) CGPA>2.75
Male	25(41.67%)	35(58.33%)
Female	27(67.5%)	13(32.5%)
Total	52(52%)	48(48%)

Source: own computation, 2006/2014
Where: LP= low performing students
HP=High performing students

Table 2 explains the academic performances of students' in accordance with their cumulative grade point average. Those students having CGPA of less than 2.5 treated as low performance in academic achievement and students scoring 2.75 and above assumed as high performance in academic achievement. As the table explores of the total 60 male respondents 25 (41.67%) of students perform poorly their CGPA is below 2.5. And the remaining 35(58.33%) of respondents performs better in academic achievement and score 2.75 and above. As far female respondents concerned 27(67.5%) of respondents out of 40 total respondents score CGPA of bellow 2.5 and poorly perform in their academic achievement. The rest 13(32.5%) of female respondents achieve better performance and score CGPA of 2.75 and above.

Table 3. Summary of the Pearson Product Moment correlation analysis for the relationship between gender of respondent and academic performance/CGPA/.

		Cumulative Grade Point Average	Gender of Respondent
Cumulative grade point average	Pearson correlation	1	.380**
	Sig. (2-tailed)		.000
	N	100	100
Gender of Respondent	Pearson correlation	.380**	1
	Sig. (2-tailed)	.000	
	N	100	100

**.Correlation is significant at the 0.01 level (2-tailed)
Source: own computation, 2006/2014

Table 3 above illustrates that the Pearson product moment correlation index obtained on the CGPA and sex of students is r = 0.380 with significance or p-value = 0.000 which is less than alpha = 0.05 implying that being maleness significantly and positively related to academic performance than females and females performed less in academic performance than male students.

Table 4. Summary of the Pearson Product Moment correlation analysis for the relationship between university admission points and academic performance/CGPA/.

		CUMULATIVE GRADE POINT AVERAGE	University Admission point
Cumulative grade point average	Pearson correlation	1	.717**
	Sig. (2-tailed)		.000
	N	100	100
University Admission point	Pearson correlation	.717**	1
	Sig. (2-tailed)	.000	
	N	100	100

**.Correlation is significant at the 0.01 level (2-tailed)
Source: own computation, 2006/2014

Table 4 above illustrates that the Pearson product moment correlation index obtained on the CGPA and university admission points is r = 0.717 with significance or p-value = 0.000 which is less than alpha = 0.05 implying that university admission points were significantly and positively related to academic performance of students /CGPA/.

Table 5. Summary of the Pearson Product Moment correlation analysis for the relationship between studying hours and academic performance/CGPA/.

		CUMULATIVE GRADE POINT AVERAGE	Studying Hours
Cumulative grade point average	Pearson correlation	1	.758**
	Sig. (2-tailed)		.000
	N	100	100
Studying Hours	Pearson correlation	.758**	1
	Sig. (2-tailed)	.000	
	N	100	100

**.Correlation is significant at the 0.01 level (2-tailed)
Source: own computation, 2006/2014

Table 5 illustrates that the Pearson product moment correlation index obtained on the CGPA and studying hours, r = 0.758 with significance or p-value = 0.000 which is less than alpha = 0.05 implying that studying hours were significantly positively related to academic performance of students /CGPA/.

4.1. Econometrics Results

This section of the paper presents the statistical significance of determinant factors of academic performance of undergraduate students obtained from linear regression (OLS).

Table 6. Regression results.

CGPA	coefficient	Std. Err.	t –value	P>|t|
AGE	.0076251	.0068714	1.11	0.270
GEN	.1645584	.049899**	3.30	0.001
AP	.0021196	.0008822**	2.40	0.018
FPEM	.00031	.0002179	1.42	0.158
ME	.0110657	.0072768	1.52	0.132
FE	.0033625	.0079622	0.42	0.674
PI	1.90e-07	2.61e-07	0.73	0.470
BTAC	-.2207531	.0776382**	-2.84	0.006
SEXP	-.1081842	.0708306	-1.53	0.130
HS	.0633419	.01691***	3.75	0.000
_cons	1.491333	.3227959***	4.62	0.000

F(10, 89) = 32.80 Prob > F = 0.0000
R-squared = 0.7865 Adj R-squared = 0.7626
Root MSE = 0.21685
Diagnostics test results
Ramsey reset test Prob>F=0.2761, F(3,86) =1
Breusch- Pagan test
Test value chi2 (10) =18.20
Prob> chi2 (10) =0.0517 Vif =2.06, 1/ Vif= 0.9
Durbin- Watson d-statistic (11,100) =1.9

, *, indicates statistical significance at 5%, 1% respectively

4.2. Econometrics Result Interpretation

The model satisfy the assumption of linearity, the assumptions of homoscedasticity or constant variance of the error term, no perfect multi co linearity among independent variables, there not be exists specification error / no functional miss specification, the assumption of normality, no serial auto correlation among successive values of the error term. Since the model satisfies the assumption of OLS, we can estimate the effect of such determinant variables on student's academic performance.

CGPA = 1.49 + 0.0076AGE + 0.1645GEN + 0.0022AP + 0.0003FPEM + .011ME + .00336FE + 0.000002PI − 0.22BTAC − .108SEXP + 0.063HS + UI (2)

The researcher assigns a value level of "1" for male respondents and assigns a value of "0" for female respondent students. And the hypothesis set in the first chapter of this paper entails that male students perform well than female students in academic success or by scoring better CGPA. The regression result also tells us the same thing with that of hypothesized in the first chapter of the paper. The regression held in favor of male students and the result also shows gender difference has significant effect on students CGPA. Male students perform well than female students. Gender difference has no effect on student's success in academic or the variation in their CGPA. Gender has positive sign and male students perform well than females. The value of the coefficient B for a variable gender is 0.1727, it entails that holding the effect of other things remain constant male students CGPA greater than female students CGPA by 0.1645.

The variable AP measures the effect of student's university

entrance exam result on their academic performance after they joined in to university. The researcher hypothesized variable AP has positive effect on student's academic performance (CGPA) after they joined in to university. AP has positive sign and significantly determines CGPA at 5% level of significance.

Parental income infers the impact of family's economic background on student's achievement in academics. The magnitude of the effect of family income on student's academic performance is found to be positive. But statistically the variable PI (parental income) has no significant effect on students CGPA.

Behaviors of students in taking alcoholic drug (BTAC) negatively significantly determine CGPA or academic performance of university students and the variable is significant at 5% level of significance. The value of the coefficient B for a variable BTAC is -0.002, it entails that holding the effect of other things remain constant if students addictiveness increased by one unit students being success or CGPA decreased by -0.22. Having sexual partnership measures how creating sexual partnership in campus affects students CGPA academic performance. Even if the variable is not statistically significant but the magnitude for its effect is negative.

Studying hour is significant positive impact on student's academic performance (CGPA). The value of the coefficient B for a variable HS is -0.063, it entails that holding the effect of other things remain constant if a student increased a studying hours by one hour a student being success or CGPA increased by 0.063.

The overall significance test prevail the combined effect of all variables included in the model best explain the dependent variable. About 79% of the variation or the change in the dependent variable or the change in CGPA is variables included in the model which is due age, gender, university admission point, former background of students regarding English and mathematics courses, socio economic background of families and students behavior in terms of having sexual partner and drug and chat habit and also studying hours.

5. Conclusions and Recommendation

After analyzing the collected information from primary respondents the researcher develops the following conclusion:

The result obtained from the Pearson product moment correlation index and the OLS regression result evidences that Gender has positive sign and male students perform well above than females. The result of this study is in contrast with the result obtained by [9]. He pointed out that gender gap in favor of male students is only related with university entrance exam scores. But in undergraduate level female students score high grade or perform better than males.

University admission point is important variable in determining student's college performance and it is significantly and positively related to academic performance of student's /CGPA/. The regression results of this study is in line with [6], found that high school grade point average is consistently the best predictor of college grade of students. And with also explains student's university entrance exam result has positive impact on CGPA of students.

The behavior of students in taking alcoholic drug and khat implying that behavior of taking alcoholic drug and khat were significantly negatively related to academic performance of students /CGPA/ with r = -0.723 and As the regression result infers t- value for variable BTAC found to be negatively significantly determine CGPA or academic performance of university students. The result obtained from the regression is in line with the hypothesis made in the first part of this paper.

The other important variable in determining student's college academic performance is studying hours. The number of hours students use to study per day significantly and positively related to academic performance of students /CGPA/ with, r = 0.758. Studying hour is significant positive impact on student's academic performance (CGPA).

Based on the study findings, the researcher recommends:
(1) Emphasis should be given to improve the academic performance of female students through adjusting special support which may allow female students perform well.
(2) Working in the ground with high school and improving students earlier before they joined in to university will be more effective so as to improve their academic achievement in college level too.
(3) Providing special support to those students coming from low income family will maintain students to achievement better.
(4) Providing Psychotherapy and supporting alcoholic drug and khat taker students to end the use of such drug and Khat will bring more fruit to improve students' academic performance.

References

[1] Agharuwhe A. Akiri 2013. Effects of Teachers' Effectiveness on Students' Academic Performance in Public Secondary Schools; Delta State - Nigeria Journal of Educational and Social Research MCSER Publishing, Rome-Italy, Vol. 3 No. 3.

[2] William saint (2004) higher education in Ethiopia; the vision and its challenge, jhea/ resa vol, 2, no. 3, 2004, pp. 8-113.

[3] The Ethiopian Ministry of Education, Education Statistics Annual Abstract 2005 E. C (2012/13).

[4] Department of International Development (DFID), United Kingdom, Ministry of Education, Federal Democratic Republic of Ethiopia, Adequacy and Effectiveness of Public Education Spending in Ethiopia (October 2010).

[5] David Bloom, David Canning, and Kevin Chan, Higher Education and Economic Development in Africa, HARVARD UNIVERSITY February 2006.

[6] Anderson, G, benjamin, D, and fuss, M 19940. determinant of success in university introductory economics courses, journal of economic education (spring, 25).

[7] International journal of information and education technology, Vol, 1, n 0-5, Dec 2011.

[8] Considire, G, and zappala, G, (2002) influence of social and economic disadvantage in the academic performance of high school students in Australia, journal of sociology, 38, 129-149 retrieved on august 16, 2007.

[9] Faroug, chaudhry, shafiq, berhanu (2011) factors affecting students quality of academic performance, university of Pakistan.

[10] Koyoshaba, marta, (2005) factors affecting academic performance of undergraduate students at Uganda Christian university.

[11] Cheesman, simpson, G. wint, (2006), determinants of student performance at university refelection from the Caribbean.

[12] Nayebzhah, Addin and Heirany, (2011) determinants of academic performance of students in four selected accounting courses at university of Zimbabwe.

[13] Yeshi mebrat, mersha, alemayehu and friew, 2013, factors affecting female students academic achievement, Bahir Dar university.

[14] S. Nayebzhah, M, moein and F, heirany, (2011) educational performance, the role background variables.

[15] The 16th international conference of Ethiopia on studies, ed by sveinege, herald aspen, birhanu tefera and shiferaw bekele, trondhein (2009).

[16] The World Bank sector study January 20, 2003, higher education development for Ethiopia; pursing the vision.

[17] Tsehaye Weldegiorgis and Yesuf Mohammed nur Awel, (2010/11) conducted their study on The Determinants of Student Attrition at College of Business and Economics, Mekelle University.

YOUR KNOWLEDGE HAS VALUE

- We will publish your bachelor's and master's thesis, essays and papers

- Your own eBook and book - sold worldwide in all relevant shops

- Earn money with each sale

Upload your text at www.GRIN.com
and publish for free